Sacred Solos

Compiled
Arranged and Edited
by CLAIR W. JOHNSON

for C Flute with Piano Accompaniment

CONTENTS

VOLUMES IN THIS SERIES

● C Flute and Piano

B♭ Clarinet and Piano

B♭ Cornet or Trumpet (Baritone 𝄞) and Piano

E♭ Alto Saxophone and Piano

Trombone or Baritone 𝄢 and Piano

Each volume varies in contents and arrangements to favor the instrument concerned.

RUBANK®

HAL•LEONARD®
CORPORATION

7777 W. BLUEMOUND RD. P.O.BOX 13819 MILWAUKEE, WI 53213

Where'er You Walk

from Semele

G. F. HANDEL
Arr. by Clair W. Johnson

Agnus Dei

GEORGES BIZET
Arr. by Clair W. Johnson

Ave Maria

FR. SCHUBERT
Arr. by Clair W. Johnson

Ave Maria 4 (Schubert)

8va to end
obbligato

(31)

Ave Maria 4 (Schubert)

If With All Your Hearts

from Elijah

FELIX MENDELSSOHN
Arr. by Clair W. Johnson

The Rosary

ETHELBERT NEVIN
Arr. by Clair W. Johnson

The Rosary 3

Calvary

PAUL RODNEY
Arr. by Clair W. Johnson

Maestoso

Andante

Giubiloso

(65) Andante

p con espressione

The Holy City

STEPHEN ADAMS
Arr. by Clair W. Johnson

SACRED SOLOS

Compiled
Arranged and Edited
by CLAIR W. JOHNSON

for C Flute with Piano Accompaniment

CONTENTS

VOLUMES IN THIS SERIES

● C Flute and Piano

B♭ Clarinet and Piano

B♭ Cornet or Trumpet (Baritone 𝄞) and Piano

E♭ Alto Saxophone and Piano

Trombone or Baritone 𝄢 and Piano

Each volume varies in contents and arrangements to favor the instrument concerned.

RUBANK®

HAL•LEONARD®
CORPORATION
7777 W. BLUEMOUND RD. P.O. BOX 13819 MILWAUKEE, WI 53213

Where'er You Walk
from Semele

G. F. HANDEL
Arr. by Clair W. Johnson

Flute

Agnus Dei

Flute

GEORGES BIZET
Arr. by Clair W. Johnson

Ave Maria

Flute

FR. SCHUBERT
Arr. by Clair W. Johnson

If With All Your Hearts

from Elijah

Flute

FELIX MENDELSSOHN
Arr. by Clair W. Johnson

The Rosary

Flute

ETHELBERT NEVIN
Arr. by Clair W. Johnson

Calvary

PAUL RODNEY
Arr. by Clair W. Johnson

The Holy City

STEPHEN ADAMS
Arr. by Clair W. Johnson

Flute

Panis Angelicus

CÉSAR FRANCK
Arr. by Clair W. Johnson

Adoration

Flute

FELIX BOROWSKI
Arr. by Clair W. Johnson

Meditation

Flute

JULES MASSENET
Arr. by Clair W. Johnson

Ave Maria

BACH-GOUNOD
Arr. by Clair W. Johnson

Alleluja
from Exsultate Jubilate

Flute

W. A. MOZART
Arr. by Clair W. Johnson

* Optional

Panis Angelicus

CÉSAR FRANCK
Arr. by Clair W. Johnson

Adoration

FELIX BOROWSKI
Arr. by Clair W. Johnson

Meditation

JULES MASSENET
Arr. by Clair W. Johnson

Meditation 4

Meditation 4

Ave Maria

BACH - GOUNOD
Arr. by Clair W. Johnson

Ave Maria 3 (Bach-Gounod)

Ave Maria 3 (Bach-Gounod)

Alleluja
from Exsultate Jubilate

W. A. MOZART
Arr. by Clair W. Johnson